Women Inventors

4

Sybilla Masters, Mary Beatrice Davidson Kenner and Mildred Davidson Austin Smith, Stephanie Kwolek, Frances Gabe

by Jean F. Blashfield

Capstone Press

MINNEAPOLIS

Printed in the United States of America.

Capstone Press • 2440 Fernbrook Lane • Minneapolis, MN 55447

Editorial Director   John Coughlan
Managing Editor   Tom Streissguth
Production Editor   James Stapleton
Book Design   Timothy Halldin
Picture Researcher   Athena Angelos

Library of Congress Cataloging-in-Publication Data

Blashfield, Jean F.
   Women inventors / by Jean F. Blashfield.
     p.   cm. -- (Capstone short biographies)
   Includes bibliographical references and index.
   Summary: Each volume presents brief accounts of five
women and their inventions.
   ISBN 1-56065-277-2
   1. Women inventors--United States--Biography--Juvenile
literature. 2. Inventions--United States--History--Juvenile
literature. [1. Inventors. 2. Inventions. 3. Women--
Biography.] I. Title. II. Series.
   T39.B53   1996
   609.2'273--dc20   95-442
   [B]   CIP
                                                          AC

Table of Contents

SEMINOLE
INDIAN V
GRINDING C
"SOFKA

Sybilla Masters
America's First Patented Inventor

She has gone down in history, but little is known about her. We would probably know nothing at all about her if her husband, Thomas Masters, had not become the mayor of the new city of Philadelphia. He had the honesty to let others know that the **patents** in his name were actually the work of his wife, Sybilla.

No one knows where or when Sybilla Righton was born. She first appeared in the colony records of New Jersey in 1692. Soon

Sybilla Masters' invention called for a machine that would drop clubs into a deep mortar, in imitation of the method used by many Native American women.

after that, she married Thomas Masters, a Quaker merchant of Philadelphia.

Off to London

In 1712, Sybilla Masters left her children and husband and went to London for a long stay. It was her plan to obtain patents for two inventions there.

Although some colonies were issuing patents, Pennsylvania did not. A British patent was more important than a colonial patent because England still ruled the colonies. The idea of patents was fairly new at the time, and there was no regular procedure. Sybilla went to see the king.

The process took several years, but she was finally granted her two patents. Both were in the name of her husband. It was generally known, however, that they were her ideas. The patents were granted by King George I, who stated publicly that the work was hers and not her husband's.

Sybilla Masters returned to Philadelphia in 1716. Her patents were published there and recorded so that they were valid in the **American colonies** as well as in England.

Her Patents

Sybilla Masters's first patent, granted in 1715, was for the process of "Cleaning and Curing the Indian Corn Growing in the severall Colonies in America." It was a process

Grinding and rolling out corn has long been an important method of cooking in the New World.

for making cornmeal, called Tuscarora rice, by a new method of grinding.

Before that, all corn had been ground like wheat, between two huge **millstones**. Sybilla Masters's method called for heavy clublike devices to drop into bowls, or mortars, holding the corn. The corn was pounded into small grains.

British patent number 401, granted to Thomas Masters, states that it is for "a new invention found out by Sybilla, his wife." Thomas Masters himself built a mill that used his wife's method of pounding corn.

Sybilla Masters is the first American woman known to have invented something. It is possible that other women may have invented things before her, but she is the first to gain public recognition for her inventions. She was also the first resident, male or female, of the American colonies to win a patent from the king of England.

Sybilla's second patent, issued in 1716, was for a method of **weaving** straw and palmetto

Early straw hats protected wearers from the rays of the sun.

leaves from the West Indies into hats and bonnets. She opened a shop in London that made and sold these popular hats, as well as chair covers of the material made by the same method.

It would be almost 100 years before an American woman received a patent in her own name. In 1809, Mary Dixon Kies of Connecticut received a patent for a new way of weaving straw with silk, also for hats.

Mary Beatrice Davidson Kenner
1912-
Mildred Davidson Austin Smith
1916-1993
Two Inventive Minds

In 1956, Mary Beatrice Davidson Kenner of Washington, D.C., was granted a patent. Her invention offered a new way of attaching a sanitary napkin to a belt for a woman to wear during her menstrual period. The device had adhesive attachments and allowed the napkin to be worn more comfortably than before.

A creative inventor, Mary Beatrice Davidson applied for patents on many practical new devices.

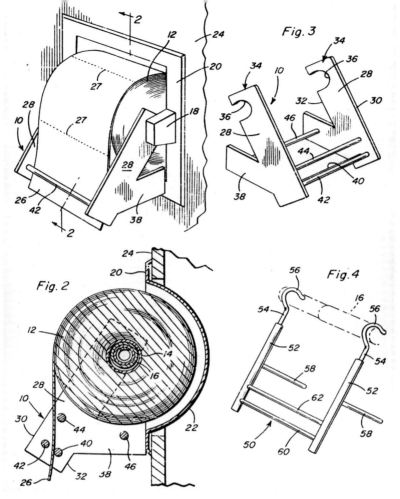

This new toilet-paper dispenser, created by Mary Beatrice, made life easier for many people.

Sadly enough, more than 30 years before, Mary Beatrice had applied for a patent for another device to be used during a woman's period. A company that originally expressed interest in her idea rejected it when they found out it had been invented by an African-American woman.

The Sisters Who Kept Thinking

Mary Beatrice Davidson and her sister, Mildred, had been inventing things since they were little girls in North Carolina. As a child, Mary Beatrice had devised a way to keep a screen door from squeaking. After Mary

Mildred Davidson joined her sister in patenting many inventions.

Beatrice married, she spent a number of years running a business before she turned to inventing again.

Mildred concentrated on music and became a professional singer. As an adult, however, she fell seriously ill with a disease called **multiple sclerosis**. When she had to spend long periods of time in bed, her creative mind began to invent again.

Neither girl had any technical education that would train them how to figure things out. They just did it. It was a trait that ran in their family. Both their father and their grandfather had had inventive minds.

It was, perhaps, Mildred's disability that made Mary Beatrice invent a special attachment to put on a walker. Many people whose legs will not support them use four-footed, lightweight walkers to walk. Mary Beatrice's attachment included a hard-surfaced tray and a soft pocket for carrying things. The patent was granted in 1976.

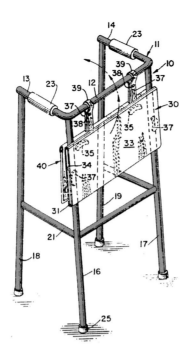

Mildred, following her own interests, invented Family Treeditions® in 1980. Family Treeditions® is a game that helps people find out about their ancestors and their family trees. Fully aware of the problems of people with disabilities, she published the game in **Braille**, too. This permitted blind people to play it. She manufactured the game and sold it herself instead of selling the rights to the game to someone else.

Mildred Davidson Austin Smith died in 1993.

Making Life Easier

Mary Beatrice has always been ready to pursue an idea that might make life easier. She patented a toilet paper holder that lets people get the tissue without having to grab for the loose end. She also devised a back scrubber that attaches to a wall in the shower or above a tub. It is certainly a lot easier than trying to get your hands around behind you to scrub your back.

There have probably been many African-American women who have invented ways to make life easier. But the Davidson sisters went ahead and applied for the patents to protect their ideas.

Stephanie Kwolek mastered the difficult process of handling supercold molecules.

Stephanie Kwolek
1923-
Mightier Than a Speeding Bullet

"Invention is invention," says chemist
Stephanie Kwolek. Creativity, or the ability to
look at things in a new way, is what is
important. It does not matter whether a woman

invents for the home or for industry. The same cleverness is needed.

While working at a chemical company, E.I. du Pont de Nemours and Company, she invented a new **fiber**, called Kevlar®. It is extraordinarily strong, five times as strong as steel. It is used on recreational boats, in outer space, and in vests worn by police confronting dangerous, armed criminals.

Putting Cold to Work

Stephanie Louise Kwolek was born in New Kensington, Pennsylvania, in 1923. She earned a college degree in chemistry and then went to work for Du Pont in 1946. She planned to stay just long enough to earn money to go to medical school. But new processes in chemistry captured her interest and she never went on to medical school.

Scientists and engineers at Dupont wear protective equipment when handling very hot or cold material.

When Kwolek started to work, chemists were just beginning to discover the many things that can be done with the chemical compounds of **petroleum**. Most plastics have been developed from petroleum.

When chemicals combine to make molecules, the molecules are usually quite small. Nature sometimes links small molecules together into long chains. These long chains

Most police departments now have a supply of Kevlar® vests, which can stop bullets.

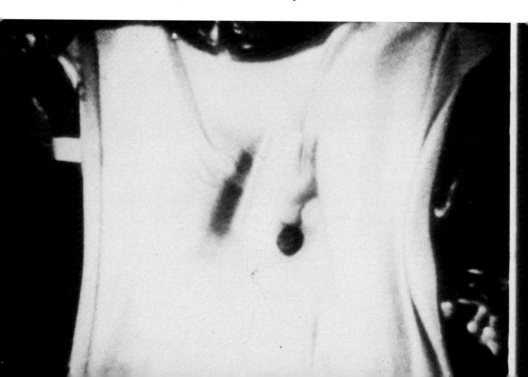

are called polymers. Starch and rubber are natural polymers.

Strange things happen to chemicals at very low temperatures. One of them is that polymers form. Kwolek and other chemists discovered that they could make artificial, or synthetic, polymers by working at very low temperatures. These polymers can be made to have special characteristics. Stephanie Kwolek learned to spin fibers from giant polymers and earned several patents in the process.

Kwolek continued to study this process for the next 40 years. Sometimes her co-workers laughed at the amount of time she spent working on these chemicals. But she became one of the most important chemists in the nation.

An Amazing Fiber

In 1966, Kwolek earned a patent for the invention of Kevlar®. It is an extra strong and extra stiff fiber. It stops bullets and is most famous for being used in vests worn by police.

It is also used in helmets that protect people in crashes. Kevlar® is a part of space vehicles, boat hulls, some automobile tires, and airplane parts.

Kevlar® earned Stephanie Kwolek the American Chemical Society's Award for Creative Invention. It also earned her a nomination to the National Inventors Hall of Fame.

Stephanie Kwolek has said that women have as much ability as men to be inventors. "You must develop the ability to notice the unusual," she says. "You must repeat and repeat and repeat until you have the problem solved."

Frances Gabe has designed many devices that are part of her self-cleaning house.

Frances Gabe
1915-
The Mystery Woman Who Hates Housework

Frances Gabe is not her real name. This woman from Newberg, Oregon, was teased so much by her neighbors that she would not allow people to write about her under her own name. Why were they laughing? Because she was determined to invent a house that would clean itself.

Sometimes Frances Gabe's name is written GABe. She made up the name out of the first letters of her real names.

This model of Gabe's self-cleaning house contains all the inventions and furniture in miniature.

Tackling a Big Job

The woman known as Frances Gabe was born near Boise, Idaho, in 1915. She was the third child of a building contractor and his wife. She was fascinated with her father's work of building houses. When she married, she used what she had learned from her father to run a building-repair company.

In her free time, Gabe wanted to play with her children, not clean house. While looking for a way to make housework easier, she remembered her father's work. She set about designing a housework-free house. It was not easy. There were many small tasks to be accomplished on the way. These smaller tasks led her to apply for as many as 68 patents over the years.

One task to be done away with was cleaning dishes. Frances Gabe invented a dish-washing cupboard. Dirty dishes put away in the cupboard came out clean for the next use. A clothes-washing closet works the same way. In this closet, a person can take a shower, too.

The model of the self-cleaning kitchen includes dozens of tiny plates, glasses, and other housewares.

Gabe's bathtub, shaped like a comfortable chair, cleans itself after the bather gets out. Her fireplace automatically dumps out ashes. Her bookshelves dust themselves.

The House That Washes Itself

After she had devised many of the separate items for the house, the Oregon Inventors Council suggested that she build the house itself. Frances Gabe's special house is 30 feet by 45 feet (9 meters by 13.5 meters), an average size for a house. But nothing else about the house is average.

Her self-cleaning house has water vents in the ceiling. Water and soap come out in a fine mist. The soap is then rinsed away with clean water. All the materials in the house, like the upholstery, are made of plastic so the water does not ruin them. After the soap has been rinsed off, blow dryers mounted in the ceilings do their work.

In the bedrooms, horizontal window shades cover the beds during washing time, because no one wants to sleep in waterproof plastic. Patented "No-Bother" lids on special plastic boxes keep papers and magazines dry.

The floors of the house are slanted so that water runs down to drains. Because all houses settle with time, Gabe built the house so that the floor's angle would adjust to the settlement.

Using what Gabe calls the General Room-Washing Apparatus takes about an hour for each room. The house-cleaning device works by the power of water alone. Expensive electricity is not needed.

Frances Gabe has been told that she is a little bit crazy and a little too far ahead of her time. But anyone who would rather do something instead of cleaning house, or who finds house-cleaning difficult, should be delighted with the idea of Gabe's work-free house.

More about Inventing

The U.S. Congress was only a year old in 1790 when it passed a law that gave people the right to stop others from copying their inventions. This is called the patent law. A patent is granted by the government for an idea for a product or a process that is original and useful.

A patent does not last forever. When the patent period is over, anyone can copy the product. A new process, new device or new plant is patented for 17 years. A design can be patented for 14 years.

When an inventor works for a company, the patent is granted in the name of the inventor.

But, he or she usually turns the right to use it over to the company.

Patents and Patenting

Suppose you have a good idea for a product. You don't want anyone to copy it. To keep that from happening, you need a patent, which says that your product is original and useful. Most important, it says that no one can make something just like it without paying you for the right to do so.

To be granted a patent, your invention must be original and useful. There are also some things it cannot be. It cannot just be a way of doing something, and it cannot be just an improvement on an older device. Also, it cannot be just written material. A book, for example, is protected by a copyright, not a patent.

What to Do with a Good Idea

You may have a bright idea for a new or improved product. You need to know how it can be produced. You also have to figure out what claims you can make for it. Are all of its parts new? What is it good for? Just how useful is it?

Many people have a lawyer help them find out whether anything about their invention is already protected by another patent. The lawyer can help an inventor file the right papers for a patent. For more information on the details of obtaining a patent, write:

Office of Information
U.S. Patent Office
Washington, D.C. 20231

or:

Canadian Intellectual Property Office
Industry Canada
Place du Portage, Phase I
50 Victoria Street
Hull, Québec K1A 0C9
Canada

WINDOW CLEANING DEVICE.

APPLICATION FILED JUNE 18, 1903.

NO MODEL.

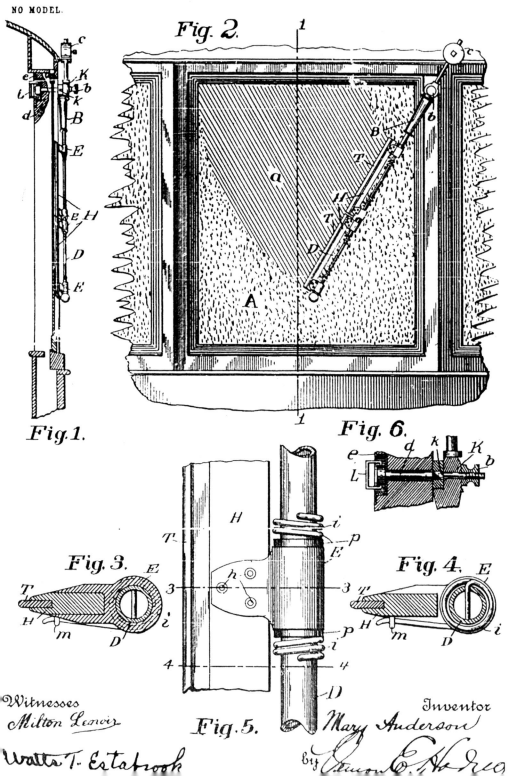

Fig. 2.

Fig. 1.

Fig. 6.

Fig. 3.

Fig. 4.

Fig. 5.

Witnesses
Milton Lenoir
Watts T. Estabrook

Inventor
Mary Anderson
by

Invent America!

The United States Patent Model Foundation is trying to find and preserve models of patented items that were made in the 19th century. But they are also trying to make sure that Americans invent new things in the 21st century.

Invent America! is their program to encourage elementary school students to think creatively. Each year since 1984, students from all over the country have submitted their inventions. Students from each region go to Washington, D.C., to vie for prizes in the national competition.

Some of the inventions created by elementary schoolchildren are unusual. One is an edible spoon for pet food, which makes it unnecessary for a pet owner to wash the spoon. Another is a disposable shield that protects the hand from a drippy paint brush. A third is a floating jigsaw puzzle for playing in a pool or the bathtub.

Mary Anderson's design for a hand-controlled windshield wiper was the first of its kind.

Glossary

American colonies–the 13 British colonies in North America that won their independence in the Revolutionary War and became the United States

Braille–a system of printing and writing for the blind, in which characters formed by patterns of raised dots are felt with the fingers

fiber–a substance that can be separated into threads or threadlike structures for spinning and weaving

millstones–a pair of large, flat, round stones between which grain and other substances are ground

multiple sclerosis–a disease that affects the central nervous system and leads to paralysis

patent–a ruling by the government that states that a certain device, or an improvement on a device, was created by a certain individual

petroleum–an oily, flammable liquid made up of a mixture of hydrocarbons, usually found beneath the earth's surface

weaving–to form by lacing together threads, yarn or strips of straw or other material

To Learn More

Aaseng, Nathan. *Twentieth-Century Inventors.* New York: Facts on File, 1991.

Bundles, A'Lelia Perry. *Madam C.J. Walker.* New York: Chelsea House Publishers, 1991.

Epstein, Vivian Sheldon. *History of Women in Science for Young People.* Denver, Colo.: VSE Publishers, 1994.

James, Portia P. *The Real McCoy: African-American Invention and Innovation, 1619-1930.* Washington, D.C.: Smithsonian Institution, 1989.

Lafferty, Peter. *The Inventor Through History.* New York: Thompson Learning, 1993.

Macaulay, David. *The Way Things Work.* Boston: Houghton Mifflin, 1988.

McKissack, Patricia and McKissack, Fredrick. *African-American Inventors.* Brookfield, Conn.: The Millbrook Press, 1994.

Pizer, Vernon. *Shortchanged by History: America's Neglected Innovators.* New York: Putnam, 1979.

Richardson, Robert O. *The Weird and Wondrous World of Patents.* New York: Sterling Publishing, 1990.

Showell, Ellen and Amram, Fred M.B. *From Indian Corn to Outer Space: Women Invent in America.* Peterborough, N.H.: Cobblestone Publishing, 1995.

Sproule, Anna. *New Ideas in Industry: Women History Makers.* New York: Hampstead Press, 1988.

Vare, Ethlie Ann and Ptacek, Greg. *Women Inventors and Their Discoveries.* Minneapolis: The Oliver Press, 1993.

Veglahn, Nancy. *Women Scientists.* New York: Facts on File, 1991.

Weiss, Harvey. *How to be an Inventor.* New York: Thomas Y. Crowell, 1980.

Yenne, Bill. *100 Inventions That Shaped World History.* San Francisco: Bluewood Books, 1993.

You can read articles about women inventors in the June 1994 issue of *Cobblestone: The History Magazine for Young People.*

Places to Visit

**Inventure Place: National Inventors
  Hall of Fame**
221 S. Broadway
Akron, OH 44308

Alabama Space and Rocket Center
Tranquillity Base
Huntsville, AL 35807

Anacostia Museum
1901 Fort Place S.E.
Washington, DC 20020

California Museum of Science and Industry
700 State Drive
Los Angeles, CA 90037

Eli Whitney Museum
945 Whitney Ave.
Hamden, CT 06517

Franklin Institute Science Museum and Planetarium
20th and Benjamin Franklin Parkway
Philadelphia, PA 19103

Museum of Science
Science Park
Boston, MA 02114

Museum of Science and Industry
57th Street and Lake Shore Drive
Chicago, IL 60637

National Air and Space Museum
Sixth and Independence Avenue S.W.
Washington, DC 20560

National Museum of American History
24th Street and Constitution Avenue N.W.
Washington, DC 20560

Some Useful Addresses

Affiliated Inventors Foundation
2132 E. Bijou St.
Colorado Springs, CO 80909-5950

Invent America!
510 King St. Suite 420
Alexandria, VA 22314

Inventors Clubs of America
Box 450261
Atlanta, GA 30345

**Inventors Workshop International
   Education Foundation**
7332 Mason Ave.
Canoga Park, CA 91306

National Inventors Foundation
345 W. Cypress St.
Glendale, CA 91204

National Women's History Project
7738 Bell Road
Windsor, CA 95492

Society of Women Engineers
120 Wall St., 11th Floor
New York, NY 10005

The Women Inventors Project
1 Greensboro Drive, Suite 302
Etobicoke, Ontario M9W 1C8
Canada

A Summer Camp for Young Inventors

Hands-on activities in science, technology, and the arts are offered at Camp Invention, a weeklong summer camp held at various sites throughout the United States. The camps, sponsored by The National Inventors Hall of Fame, are for students in grades one through five. A companion program, Camp Ingenuity, was recently launched for students in grades six through eight. For information, call 1-800-968-4332.

Index

Photo credits: Collection of Jim Davie, US Patent & Trademark Office, p. 17; Collection of Patricia Ives Sluby: pp. 10, 13; DuPont: pp. 18, 20; Contributed by Frances Gabe, SCH Studios: cover, pp. 23, 24, 26, 27; Library of Congress Prints & Photo Division: pp. 4, 7, 9; US Patent & Trademark Office: pp. 12, 32